Hello!
I am a Beaver.

I0108771

Capybaras are a bit bigger than me.

Beaver's are the second largest rodents in the world.

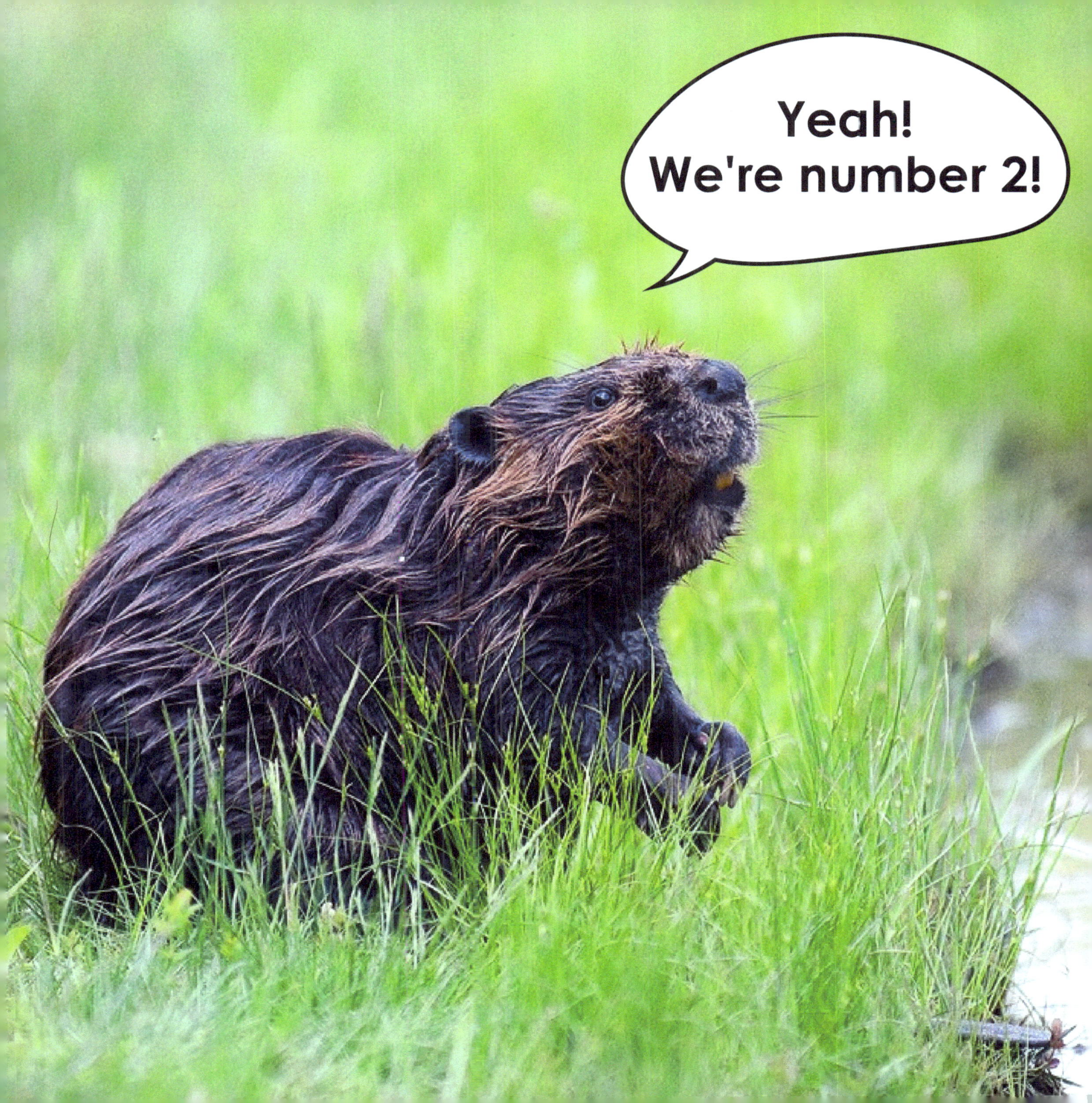
Yeah!
We're number 2!

Beavers use their big, flat tails
to turn better in the water.

Beaver tails are also useful for warning other beavers of danger by slapping the water surface.

Be careful, everyone!

I chew on wood to stop my teeth from getting too long.

Beavers have sharp, orange-colored teeth that never stop growing.

My home is called a "lodge".

Beavers build dams and lodges using sticks, mud, and rocks.

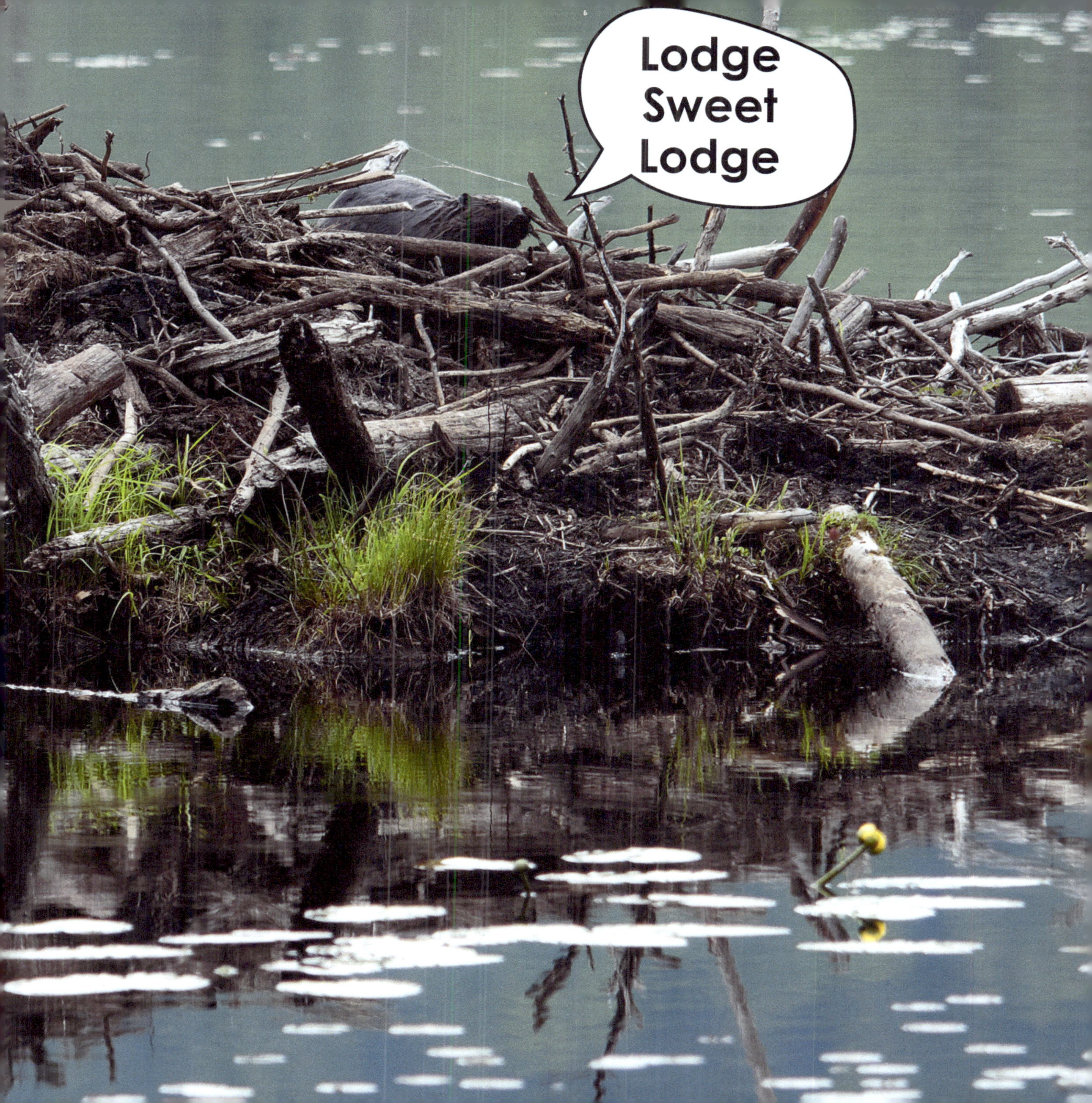
Lodge
Sweet
Lodge

Beavers build their lodges in the water, and the entrance is underwater.

My secret underwater entrance keeps me safe from predators.

Beavers are expert swimmers.

They can stay under water and hold their breath for up to 15 minutes.

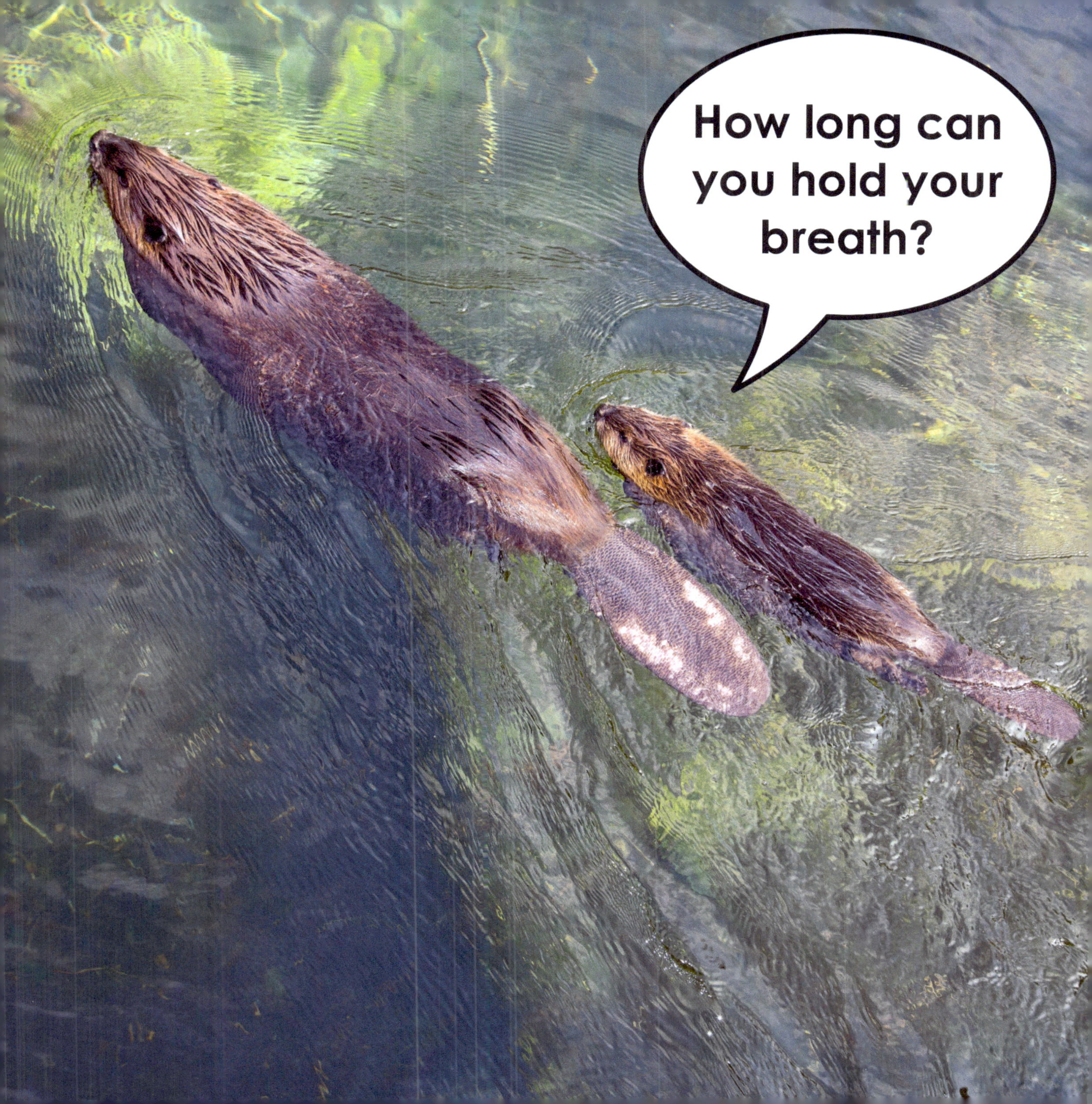
How long can you hold your breath?

Beavers paddle through the water at speeds up to 5 miles (8 km) per hour.

I have 2 different layers of fur.

The outer layer is thick and waterproof. It keeps the beaver dry when it's in the water.

The under layer is called "beaver wool". It's soft and keeps the beaver warm.

Beavers are mostly nocturnal. That means they are most active at night.

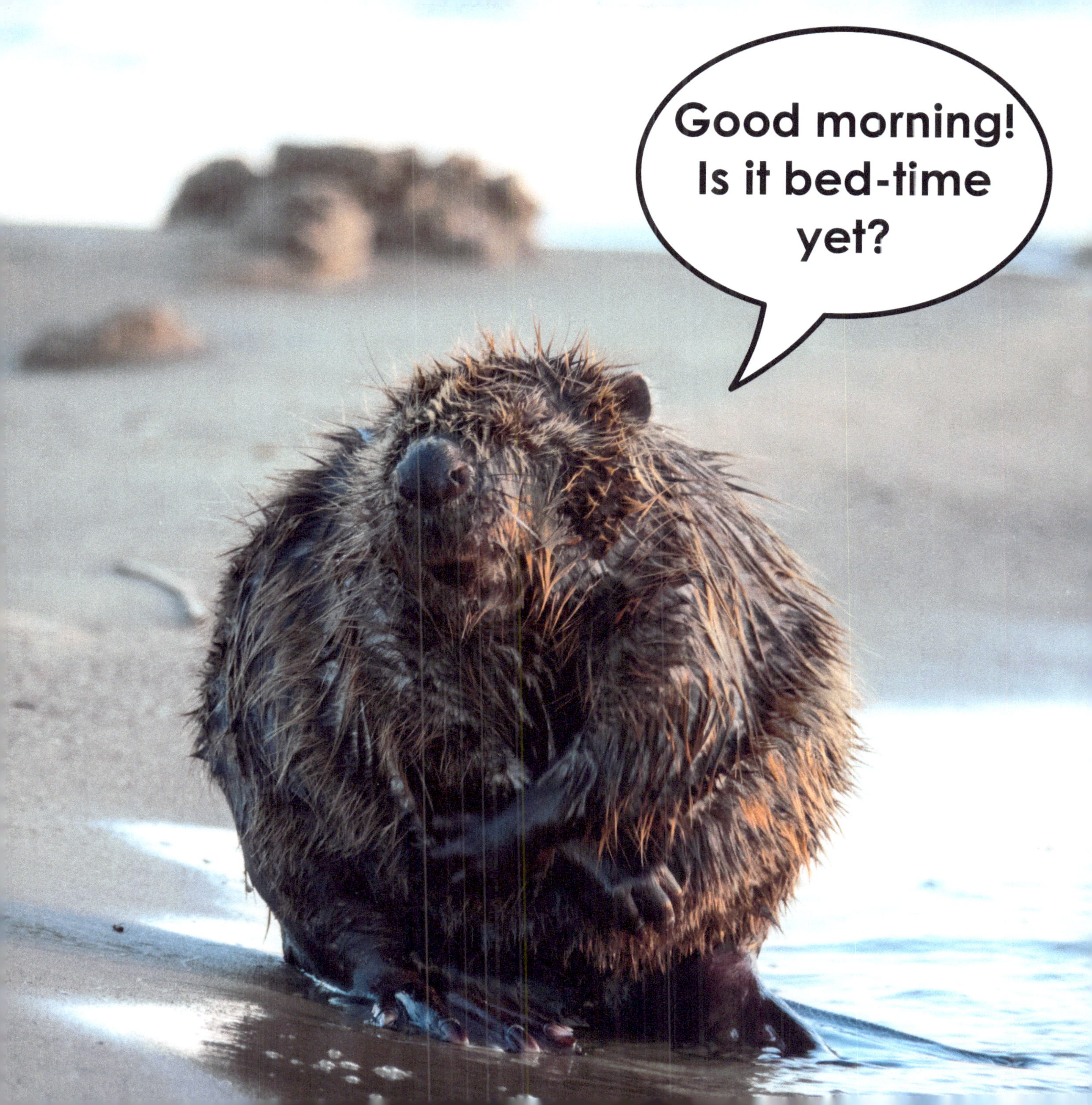
Good morning!
Is it bed-time
yet?

A "herbivore" is an animal that only eats plants.

I am a herbivore.

We love eating bark, leaves, and twigs of trees.

Beavers have a strong, musky odor. It helps them communicate with other beavers.

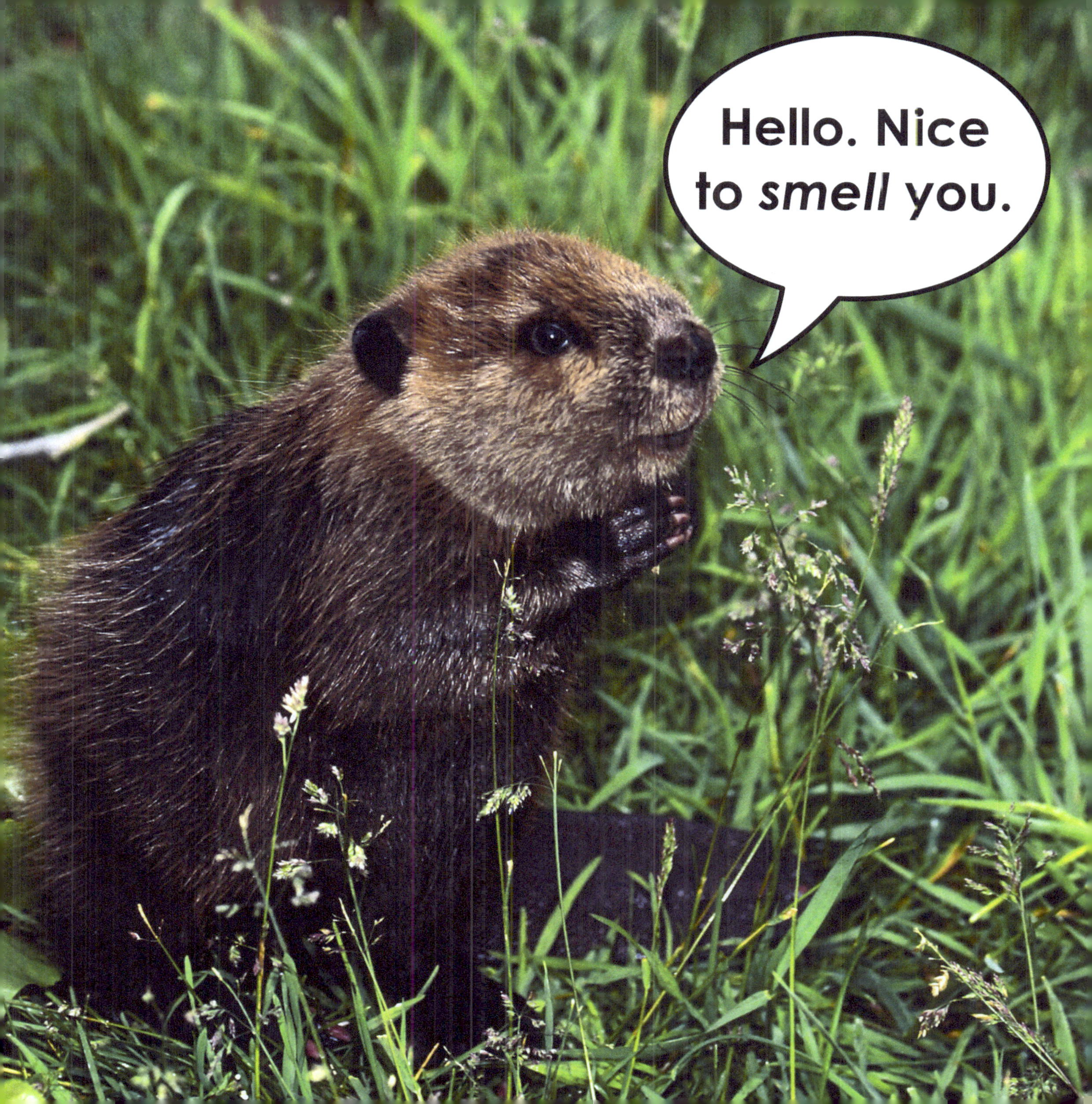
Hello. Nice to *smell* you.

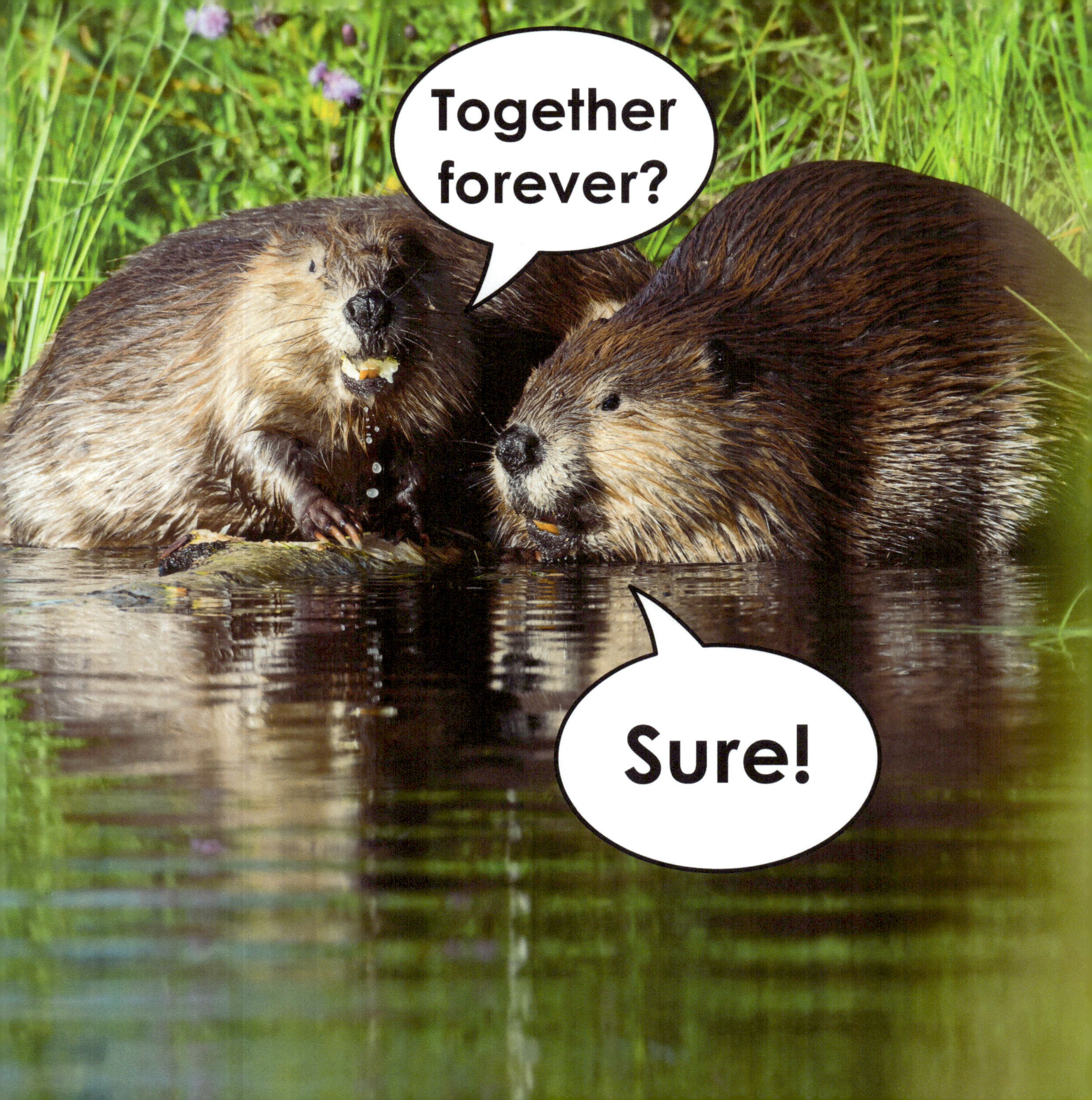
Together forever?
Sure!

Beavers are "monogamous".

That means they only have one mate for their whole life.

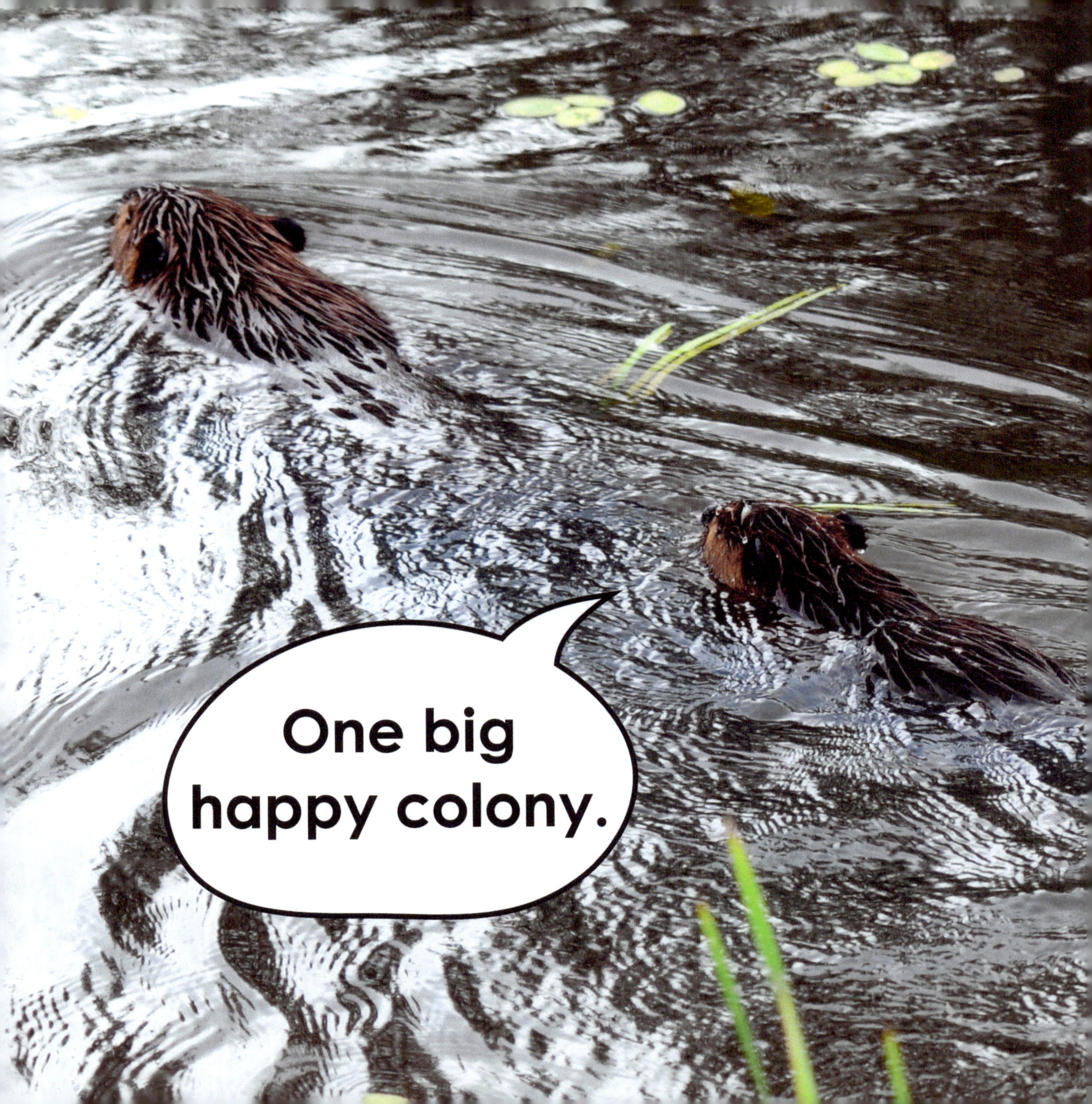
One big
happy colony.

A beaver family group is called a "colony".

Baby beavers are called "kits".

They are born with all their fur
and their eyes open.

Beavers have a strong sense of smell. It helps them find food and detect danger.

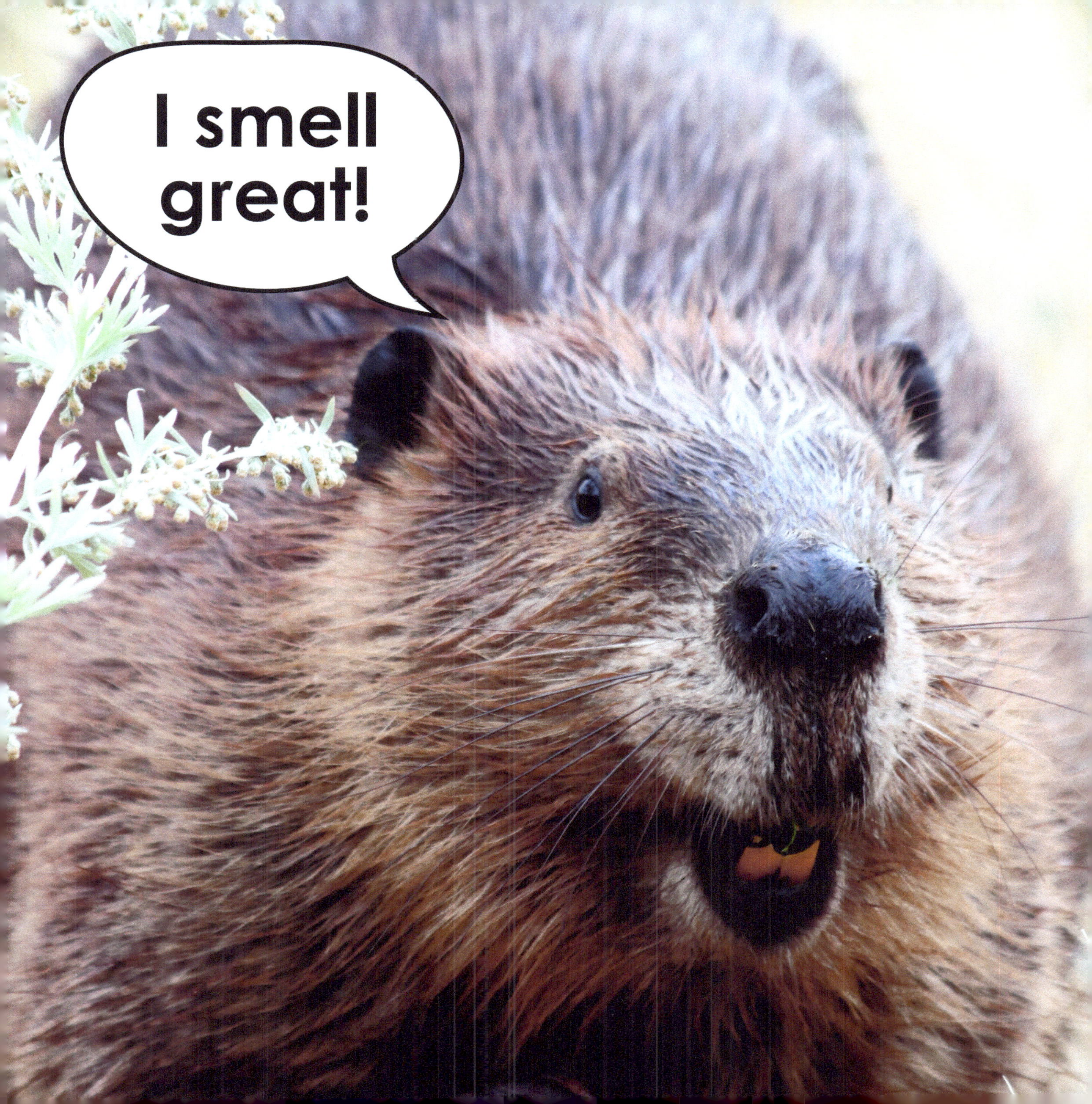
I smell great!

Hello parents!

Visit us to find out about new releases and *FREE* offers. We'll let you know when we have a new release coming out and how you can get it for FREE.
And you can cast your vote for what book we make next!

scan here

or visit here

ActiveBrainsBooks.com

---

scan here

Let us know what you think. As an independent publisher, your honest reviews mean a lot to us and our business. We'd love to hear from you!

amazon.com/review/create-review/

or visit here

FOLLOW US on Amazon.

amazon.com/author/activebrainsbooks

ActiveBrainsBooks.com

ACTIVE
BRAINS

www.ingramcontent.com/pod-product-compliance
Lightning Source LLC
Chambersburg PA
CBHW042056040426

42447CB00003B/249